MINERALS ROCKS & FOSSILS

This book belongs to:

Iain Anderson

Cambrian (570-500 mya)
So-called after the Latin name for Wales, where rocks of this period were first thoroughly studied, the Cambrian seas offered conditions in which life could begin to diversify. Rocks of this age may contain abundant fossils, especially trilobites.

Ordovician (500-435 mya)
Trilobites still flourished in the seas and the first backboned animals made their appearance. The *Ordovices* were an ancient British tribe of people who once lived in North Wales where geologists studied the rocks of this age.

Silurian (435-408 mya)
As well as corals and other creatures, the first jawed fishes appeared. The *Silures* were another British tribe who lived in Wales where rock samples of the period are abundant.

Devonian
(408-360 mya)
Named after the English county of Devon, this Period is often known as the 'age of the fishes' because it was at this time, the first fishes with backbones evolved.

Carboniferous
(360-285 mya)
It was during the 'coal age' that insects and reptiles made their appearance. Coal was formed in the vast areas of coastal swamps that existed in the later part of the Period.

Permian
(285-245 mya)
During this Period the numbers and types of reptiles increased. Perm is a town in Russia. Rocks of this age were studied nearby.

All the reconstructions on these pages were made by the famous Czech artist Zdenek Burian

Triassic
(245-208 mya)
This period is so named because scientists were able to divide the rocks into three distinct groups. The first dinosaurs, flying reptiles, and mammals appeared.

Jurassic
(208-144 mya)
Named after the Jura Mountains, this Period is also called the 'age of reptiles' when dinosaurs dominated the Earth, and the first birds appeared.

Cretaceous
(144-65 mya)
The 'age of chalk'; in the warm deep seas of the period the tiny skeletons of countless sea creatures were accumulating as chalky sediments. At the end of this period, dinosaurs, pterosaurs, and many other groups of animals suddenly died out.

Words in SMALL CAPITAL LETTERS are defined elsewhere in the glossary.

bedding the sheet-like layers in which sedimentary rocks are deposited.
corallite the skeleton that is formed by and supports an individual coral.
country rock the ROCK into which an INTRUSION has been thrust.
cross-cutting describes an igneous rock that cuts across the surrounding COUNTRY ROCKS.
crystal a natural solid with regularly arranged plane faces that are in keeping with the arrangement of the atoms from which the crystal is made.
dyke a wall-like body of igneous rock that CROSS-CUTS the COUNTRY ROCKS. Dykes may be vertical or almost vertical.
fibrous a term used to describe the form of a MINERAL. A fibrous mineral appears to be made of thread-like strands.
fossil any trace or remains of an animal or plant that lived thousands or millions of years ago.
fossiliferous containing FOSSILS.
gemstone a MINERAL in which the colour, hardness, and clearness are such that it can be cut and polished for decorative purposes.
geode a hollow, stony object which, when broken open, reveals good-quality CRYSTALS, often of quartz, growing usually from the outside towards the centre.
geyser a VENT which, from time to time, spouts a jet of boiling water.
grade the quality of an ORE; the amount by which a ROCK has been metamorphosed; the part of a sedimentary rock in which the grains are consistent size eg sand grade.
granular describing the form of a MINERAL that is made up of grains.
intrusion a body of igneous rock that has been thrust into existing COUNTRY ROCKS.
lava molten rock erupted by a volcano.
lode VEINS of MINERALS, usually of economically valuable ORES.
lustre the way in which a MINERAL reflects light, its sheen.
massive describing a MINERAL that occurs as a formless lump.
matrix the material in a rock that contains the larger grains or CRYSTALS.
mineral a naturally occurring substance with a crystalline structure and a definite chemical composition.
mineral, replacement a MINERAL that has replaced the mineral that first formed.
mineral, rock-forming any of the MINERALS, such as quartz or feldspar, that make up the bulk of all ROCKS.
ore a MINERAL or a ROCK from which useful materials, such as iron or copper, can be extracted economically.
ornament the ridges, knobs, or other features on a fossil shell.
rhomb short for rhombohedron. A six-faced crystal form.
rock an aggregate of MINERALS.
shale a fine-grained sedimentary rock with a flaky structure.
sill a table-like INTRUSION which has been thrust into the COUNTRY ROCK roughly parallel with its BEDDING.
sorting in a sedimentary ROCK, the amount by which the grains or fragments have been sorted into similar sizes; eg a poorly sorted rock has grains of many different sizes.
stalactite a long, icicle-like body of limestone hanging down from the ceiling of a cavern.
vein a table-like body of MINERALS contained in a fracture in the ROCKS.
vent a tear in the Earth's crust through which LAVA, ash, hot fluids, and gas erupt.
whorl one of the turns of a spiral shell.

Note: the colour of a mineral may be misleading, but its colour in powdered form is helpful in identification. The simplest way of obtaining this is to scratch the mineral across a piece of white, unglazed porcelain. This is called the mineral's streak and the piece of porcelain is known as a streak plate.

Gold

Natural form: cubic crystals; found as loose grains or as nuggets, or as delicate, frond-like structures called dendrites. ***Hardness:*** can be scratched with a knife. ***Colour:*** golden yellow with a similar streak. ***Found:*** in North Wales and Scotland in veins associated with quartz, or in river or stream deposits if weathered from the mother lode; rare. ***Uses:*** jewellery.
I-Spy for ***50***

Silver

Natural form: cubic crystals; often found as wiry or scaly growths. ***Hardness:*** can be scratched with a knife. ***Colour:*** silver stains to black; silver-white streak; metallic lustre. ***Found:*** in veins, in south-west England, for example. ***Uses:*** like gold, it can be beaten and shaped. It is used to make jewellery and in photographic film.
I-Spy for ***50***

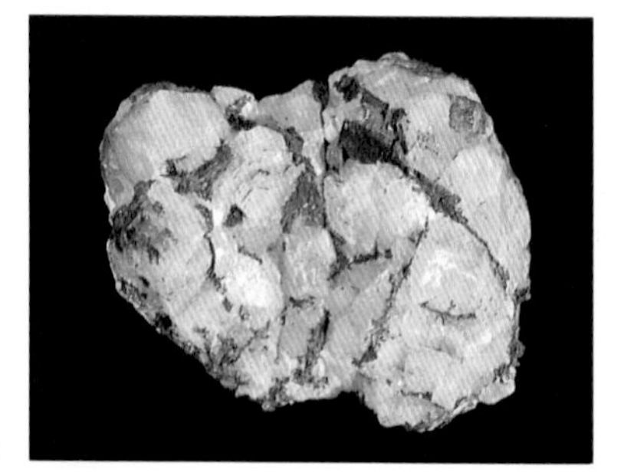

Copper

Natural form: cubic crystals; often found as plant-like dendrites or as cubes.***Hardness:*** may be scratched with a knife. ***Colour:*** red-brown tarnishes to dull brown; copper-red streak; metallic lustre. ***Found:*** throughout certain sandstones, breccias, or conglomerates, and in association with basalts in areas such as the Pennines and North Wales. ***Uses:*** in the building industry.
I-Spy for ***30***

Sulphur

Natural form: tabular crystals or crystals resembling pyramids joined base to base. ***Hardness:*** can be scratched with a finger nail. ***Colour:*** bright yellow, sometimes with a brown tinge; white streak; resin-like lustre. ***Found:*** in volcanic areas as masses round vents and in fractures in limestones. ***Uses:*** in the manufacture of sulphuric acid, matches, and in some insecticides.

I-Spy for ***20***

Graphite

Natural form: massive lumps or table-shaped crystals. ***Hardness:*** may be marked with a finger nail. ***Colour:*** black; black streak; dull, metallic sheen. ***Found:*** in rocks changed by temperature and/or pressure, such as in schists, and in pegmatite veins. ***Uses:*** in making pencils and in the electricity industry. Graphite is sometimes wrongly given the name of a heavy metal. Which metal?

I-Spy for ***30*** *— double with answer*

Pyrite

Natural form: cubic crystals. ***Hardness:*** difficult to scratch with a knife; will mark glass. ***Colour:*** brassy or golden yellow; black streak; metallic lustre. ***Found:*** in association with igneous rocks; in black shales as cubes or nodules; or in mineral veins; widespread. Pyrite fractures easily and weathers quickly. ***Uses:*** in the manufacture of sulphuric acid; ornamental. Because it resembles a precious metal, what name is sometimes given to pyrite?

I-Spy for ***10*** *— double with answer*

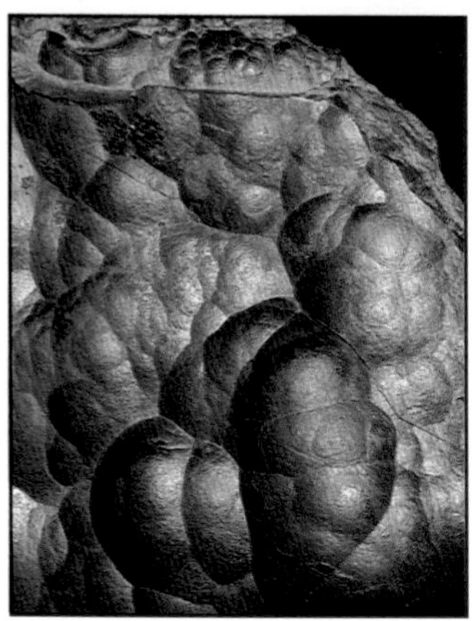

Galena

Natural form: cubic; may also be massive or granular. ***Hardness:*** can be scratched with a knife. ***Colour:*** dull lead grey; dull grey streak; metallic lustre. ***Found:*** in veins and in sedimentary rocks that have been soaked with hot fluids rising from the inner Earth, in areas such as south-west England, the Pennines, and Scotland. ***Uses:*** an important lead ore.
I-Spy for ***20***

Haematite

Natural form: tabular crystals, rose-like growths, and domed masses (kidney ore). ***Hardness:*** can be marked with a knife but will just scratch glass. ***Colour:*** reddish black, steel grey, black; dark-red streak; metallic lustre. ***Found:*** usually in sandstones and limestones affected by mineral-rich fluids; widespread. ***Uses:*** as an iron ore, and in stains and pigments.
I-Spy for ***20***

Corundum

Natural form: barrel-shaped, pyramid-like, or tabular crystals. ***Hardness:*** very hard, will scratch glass. ***Colour:*** brown to blue-grey; ruby and sapphire (varieties) are red and blue respectively; glassy lustre. ***Found:*** in pegmatite veins and metamorphic rocks; gems may occur in river or stream deposits; rare. ***Uses:*** as an abrasive; gemstones in jewellery.
I-Spy for ***50***

Cassiterite

Natural form: pyramid-like crystals or massive ore deposit. ***Hardness:*** will scratch glass. ***Colour:*** black or red-brown; white-grey streak; slightly metallic sheen. ***Found:*** associated with pegmatite veins and near granite intrusions; in south-west England, for example. ***Uses:*** an important ore of tin; also known as tinstone.
*I-Spy for **40***

Goethite

Natural form: prisms or tabular crystals. ***Hardness:*** can be scratched with a knife. ***Colour:*** dark to yellow-brown; yellow streak; dull lustre. ***Found:*** in weathered zones of iron-rich deposits, in iron mines, for example. ***Uses:*** an ore of iron.
*I-Spy for **40***

Halite

Natural form: cubes and as massive deposits of rock salt. ***Hardness:*** can just be scratched with a finger nail. ***Colour:*** colourless, white, and yellow, sometimes red and blue; white streak; glassy lustre. ***Found:*** associated with the evaporation of salt-water brines, found as layered deposits; in the English Midlands, for example. ***Uses:*** in the manufacture of hydrochloric acid and in foods.
*I-Spy for **30***

Fluorite

Natural form: mostly cubes but sometimes rhomb-like. ***Hardness:*** can be scratched with a knife. ***Colour:*** yellow, blue, green, purple, and even black; white streak; glassy lustre. ***Found:*** in mineral veins in limestone areas associated with quartz, barytes, and galena; in the Pennines and the Lake District, for example. ***Uses:*** in smelting; ornamental.

I-Spy for ***30***

Calcite

Natural form: prisms, rhomb-like crystals, and fibres. Dog-tooth spar is a very common form. ***Hardness:*** easily scratched with a knife. ***Colour:*** colourless or white if pure, various colours if stained; white streak; glassy lustre. ***Found:*** as crystals in veins, but is an important mineral in limestones and as a cement; widespread. ***Uses:*** in the cement industry; smelting; fertilizers.

I-Spy for ***10***

Siderite

Natural form: rhomb-like crystals with curved faces; may also be fibrous or massive. ***Hardness:*** can be scratched with a knife. ***Colour:*** grey, yellow-brown; white streak; glassy lustre. ***Found:*** as clay ironstone and in veins, in areas such as the Midlands and Pennines. ***Uses:*** iron ore.

I-Spy for ***40***

Dolomite

Natural form: rhomb-like crystals with curved faces, or as a rock-forming mineral. ***Hardness:*** can be scratched with a knife. ***Colour:*** colourless, white, pink, or yellow-brown; white streak; pearly to glassy lustre. ***Found:*** widespread as a rock-forming mineral. ***Uses:*** building stone and for making furnace bricks. Where are the Dolomite Mountains?

*I-Spy **10** for dolomite rock*
Double with answer

Aragonite

Natural form: needle-like and tabular crystals; the crystals often occur as twins. ***Hardness:*** can be scratched with a knife. ***Colour:*** colourless, white, yellowish to grey; white streak; glassy lustre. ***Found:*** in crystal form in veins and cavities, and in the structure of some sea shells; with time it is an unstable mineral so that it is found only rarely in ancient fossil shells; south-west England, for example.
*I-Spy for **40***

Malachite

Natural form: rounded banded masses, or as fibres. ***Hardness:*** can be scratched with a knife. ***Colour:*** bright green; pale-green streak; dull to silky sheen. ***Found:*** associated with oxidized copper deposits; North Wales, for example. ***Uses:*** as a source of copper, jewellery, ornamental.
*I-Spy for **40***

Baryte

Natural form: tabular, or as diamond-shaped prisms; fibrous, or as cock's-comb masses. ***Hardness:*** easily scratched by a knife. ***Colour:*** colourless, white, or stained by impurities; white streak; glassy to pearly lustre. ***Found:*** in veins associated with copper, zinc, iron, and nickel; widespread. ***Uses:*** in paint and textile industries; as a drilling mud in the oil industry; 'barium meal' in hospital investigations.
*I-Spy for **10***

Gypsum

Natural form: tabular crystals with curved faces; fibrous, massive, or granular. ***Hardness:*** can be scratched with a finger nail. ***Colour:*** colourless, white, or possibly yellow, grey, or brown if stained by impurities; white streak; glassy, pearly, or dull lustre. ***Found:*** in areas where sea water has evaporated, or as desert roses; widespread. ***Uses:*** to make plaster of Paris, fertilizers.
*I-Spy for **10***

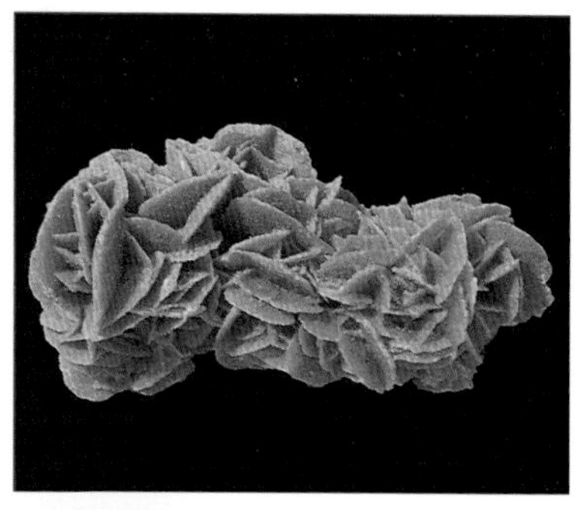

Apatite

Natural form: tabular or prism-shaped crystals. ***Hardness:*** can be scratched with a knife. ***Colour:*** green, yellow, white, brown, possibly tinged with red or blue; white streak; glassy lustre. ***Found:*** in veins and in association with pegmatites, bedded phosphates, and in fossil bones; widespread. ***Uses:*** to make fertilizers.
*I-Spy for **40***

Vanadinite

Natural form: short or long prisms, needle-like, or globular. ***Hardness:*** will scratch glass. ***Colour:*** orange-red, brown-red, and yellow; white, yellow-white streak; glassy lustre. ***Found:*** in association with lead minerals, sometimes in limestone; rare. ***Uses:*** in the manufacture of steel.

I-Spy for ***50***

Lazulite

Natural form: double pyramid crystals, stone-like masses. ***Hardness:*** will just scratch glass. ***Colour:*** light blue or azure blue; white streak; glassy lustre. ***Found:*** in association with quartz and pegmatites; rare. ***Uses:*** semi-precious stone, in jewellery and ornamental.

I-Spy for ***50***

Olivine

Natural form: as grains in basalts or as poorly shaped masses. ***Hardness:*** will scratch glass. ***Colour:*** olive green, white, yellow-brown, or black. ***Found:*** in rocks low in quartz, such as basalt and gabbro; widespread. ***Uses:*** in the manufacture of high-temperature bricks; semi-precious stone (peridot).

I-Spy for ***30***

Hornblende

Natural form: long or short prisms, or as granular or fibrous masses. ***Hardness:*** will just scratch a knife blade. ***Colour:*** shades of green to almost black; glassy lustre. ***Found:*** in igneous rocks and some metamorphic rocks that have undergone change through medium grades of pressure and temperature; widespread.
*I-Spy for **30***

Zircon

Natural form: prisms ending in double pyramids. ***Hardness:*** will scratch glass. ***Colour:*** brown, reddish brown, less commonly yellow, green, or violet; white streak; glassy lustre. ***Found:*** in association with pegmatite veins and as a minor mineral in granites and syenites; south-west England and Scotland, for example. ***Uses:*** gemstone.
*I-Spy for **40***

Garnet

Natural form: rhomb-like crystals or massive. ***Hardness:*** will scratch glass. ***Colour:*** varies with type, eg pyrope is deep red to black, uvarovite clear green; glassy or resin-like lustre. ***Found:*** in association with schists, gneisses (almandine), serpentinites (pyrope), granites and pegmatites (spessartine); the Lake District and Scotland, for example. ***Uses:*** in abrasives and as gemstones.
*I-Spy for **20***

Andalusite

Natural form: prisms or crystals that are square in cross-section. ***Hardness:*** will scratch glass. ***Colour:*** usually pink or red, but brown, green, and grey forms have been found. ***Found:*** in association with fine-grained metamorphic rocks and pegmatite veins; in Scotland, for example. ***Uses:*** in spark plugs for the motor industry; clear green variety used as a gemstone. After a province in which European country was this mineral named?

I-Spy for ***20*** *— double with answer*

Topaz

Natural form: prisms or massive. ***Hardness:*** almost as hard as diamond, will scratch glass. ***Colour:*** usually pale yellow, blue, or less commonly green or pink. ***Found:*** in quartz veins, granite pegmatites, or rhyolites; rare. ***Uses:*** as a gemstone.

I-Spy for ***50***

Tourmaline

Natural form: long prisms with furrowed faces; triangular in cross-section. ***Hardness:*** will scratch glass. ***Colour:*** often black, but green, blue, brown, and pink varieties have been found. ***Found:*** in granite pegmatites, gneisses, and schists; in south-west England, the Lake District, and Scotland. ***Uses:*** in the electrical industry and as a gemstone.

I-Spy for ***30***

Epidote

Natural form: this is a group of minerals that occur in prisms or show a tabular crystal form. ***Hardness:*** varies slightly but most are harder than a knife blade. ***Colour:*** variable; epidote is green to black. ***Found:*** epidote is found in many metamorphic rocks that have been affected by low-grade temperature and pressure changes; Scotland, for example. ***Uses:*** rarer forms are of gemstone quality.

I-Spy for ***40***

Beryl

Natural form: prisms with furrowed long faces. ***Hardness:*** will scratch glass. ***Colour:*** white, yellow, green, pink, orange, and blue; white streak; glassy lustre. ***Found:*** associated with granite pegmatites, veins, schists, and gneisses. ***Uses:*** a source of beryllium; gemstone (emerald etc).

I-Spy for ***50***

Augite

Natural form: massive or granular, or as prisms that are square in cross-section. ***Hardness:*** can not be scratched with a knife. ***Colour:*** dark green, black; white streak; glassy lustre. ***Found:*** in igneous rocks that have a low quartz content.

I-Spy for ***40***

Mica

Natural form: dark mica (biotite) or light mica (muscovite); flexible flakes. ***Hardness:*** easily scratched with a knife. ***Colour:*** muscovite colourless, green, or pale brown; biotite dark brown, greenish black, or black. ***Found:*** in many igneous and metamorphic rocks; widespread. ***Uses:*** in the electrical industry.
I-Spy for ***10***

Talc

Natural form: granular or 'banded' masses; crystals uncommon. ***Hardness:*** very soft. ***Colour:*** white, pale green; white streak; soapy feel and dull lustre. ***Found:*** in association with schists; widespread. ***Uses:*** as talcum powder, filler, soapstone, and in the ceramics industries.
I-Spy for ***30***

Quartz

Natural form: commonly as six-sided prisms; massive in veins. ***Hardness:*** cannot be scratched with a knife. ***Colour:*** usually colourless or white; semi-precious varieties are coloured, eg rose quartz, citrine, smoky quartz. ***Found:*** abundant in many rocks; widespread. ***Uses:*** quartz sand in the building industry, abrasives, semi-precious stones.
I-Spy for ***10***

Agate

Natural form: layered and banded in rings; often forms hollow nodules called geodes; it is a form of quartz. ***Hardness:*** as quartz. ***Colour:*** colourless to highly coloured. ***Found:*** common in volcanic lavas; in Scotland, for example. ***Uses:*** ornamental and semi-precious stone.

*I-Spy for **40***

Opal

Natural form: rounded, massive, stalactite-like forms, or as a replacement mineral. ***Hardness:*** harder than a knife blade. ***Colour:*** variable, colourless, milky white, red, brown, blue, green and black. ***Found:*** in association with hot springs and geysers; may fill cavities in rocks, formed at low temperatures; rare. ***Uses:*** gemstone; one form used as an abrasive.

*I-Spy for **50***

Orthoclase feldspar

Natural form: short, 'flattened' prisms. ***Hardness:*** cannot be scratched with a knife. ***Colour:*** white to pale pink; white streak; lustre pearly to glassy. ***Found:*** abundant in granites, microgranites, and many other igneous and metamorphic rocks.

*I-Spy for **20***

Plagioclase feldspar

Natural form: prisms and as tabular crystals. ***Hardness:*** as orthoclase. ***Colour:*** white, less commonly pink or with green or brown colouring; white streak; lustre pearly to glassy. ***Found:*** abundant in many igneous rocks; widespread. ***Uses:*** in the ceramics industry.
I-Spy for ***20***

Analcime (Analcite)

Natural form: granular or massive. Hardness: can just be scratched by a knife. ***Colour:*** pink, white, grey, yellow, green; white streak; glassy lustre. ***Found:*** south-west England, Scotland. ***Uses:*** in chemical industries.
I-Spy for ***50***

Chrysotile (asbestos)

Natural form: fibrous, platy, or layered. ***Hardness:*** easily scratched with a knife. ***Colour:*** white, yellow, various greens; colourless streak; waxy to pearly lustre. ***Found:*** as a minor mineral in igneous rocks, notably in serpentinites; in Scotland, for example. ***Uses:*** fire protection.
I-Spy for ***40***

Igneous rocks are those rocks that have crystallized out from magma (molten rock) as it has cooled.

Granite

Grain size: coarse to very coarse. ***Colour:*** white, pink, or grey. ***Texture:*** often with well-shaped crystals of feldspar; quartz, biotite, muscovite. ***Found:*** often cross-cuts country rocks in areas of ancient rocks; south-west England, Scotland, the Lake District. ***Uses:*** kerb stones, facing stone. Which city in Scotland is known as 'the granite city'?

*I-Spy for **10** — double with answer* ☐

Granite pegmatite

Grain size: very coarse to gigantic. ***Colour:*** uneven or patchy; mostly white, pink, or red. ***Texture:*** large to huge crystals roughly parallel to one another. ***Found:*** as cross-cutting dykes near granite intrusions; south-west England and Scotland, for example.

*I-Spy for **20*** ☐

Syenite

Grain size: coarse to very coarse. ***Colour:*** similar to granites or slightly darker. ***Texture:*** grains tend to be of equal size. Crystals are mostly feldspars with no more than 10% quartz. ***Found:*** as cross-cutting dykes and as sills; in Scotland, for example.

*I-Spy for **30*** ☐

Diorite

Grain size: coarse, sometimes with large crystal growths. ***Colour:*** speckled black and white, sometimes with a pink or green tinge. ***Texture:*** equal grain size but large crystals may have developed. ***Found:*** as individual intrusions; south-west England, North Wales, the Lake District, Scotland. ***Uses:*** facing stone.

*I-Spy for **10***

Gabbro

Grain size: coarse. ***Colour:*** from grey to black but may have green and blue tinge. ***Texture:*** grains obvious, often of equal size; rock may be layered with zones of light and dark minerals. Minerals mainly plagioclase feldspar, quartz, olivine, or hornblende. ***Found:*** in areas of ancient country rock as cross-cutting intrusions; south-west England, the Lake District, Scotland. ***Uses:*** facing stone.

*I-Spy for **20***

Serpentinite

Grain size: medium to coarse. ***Colour:*** green, grey-green to black. ***Texture:*** waxy appearance, sometimes with a splintery fracture. Minerals mainly olivine, hornblende, pyroxene, and mica. ***Found:*** as cross-cutting intrusions. Serpentinites are formed mostly by the alteration of other rocks. In south-west England and Scotland, for example. ***Uses:*** ornaments and as facing stone.

*I-Spy for **20***

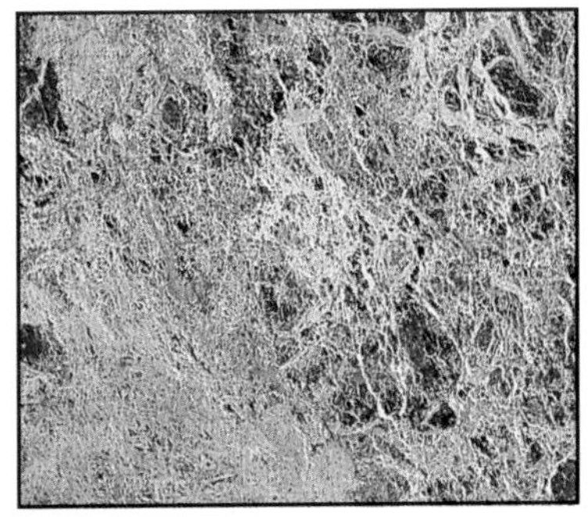

Microgranite

Grain size: individual crystals medium sized but larger, well-formed quartz and feldspar crystals may stand out. ***Colour:*** speckled white, grey, pink. ***Texture:*** may show flow features, with crystals parallel to one another. ***Found:*** as intrusions or veins; south-west England, the Lake District, Scotland. ***Uses:*** road stone, kerbstones.
*I-Spy for **10***

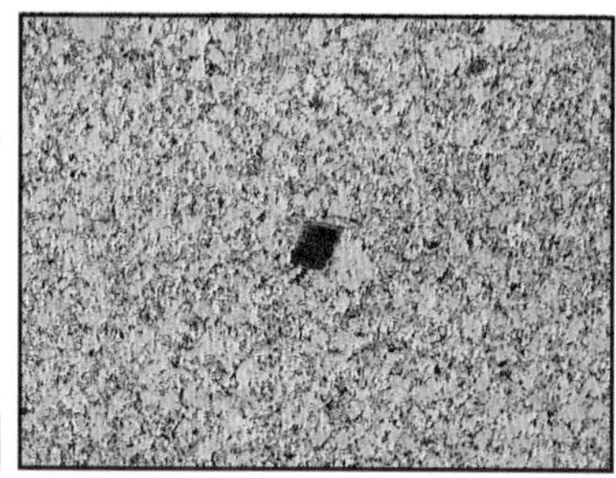

Rhyolite

Grain size: fine to very fine. ***Colour:*** pale coloured, white, grey, or green, sometimes red or brown. ***Texture:*** may be layered or banded, often with rounded hollow spaces (vesicles formed by gas bubbles). ***Found:*** as lava flows or dykes; south-west England, North Wales, the Lake District, Scotland. ***Uses:*** building stone, decorative stone.
*I-Spy for **20***

Obsidian/Pitchstone

Grain size: none – the rock looks glassy. ***Colour:*** black, brown, or grey with a glass-like shine. ***Texture:*** rare to common small crystals may occur in the glassy mass. ***Found:*** lava flows and dykes; North Wales, the Lake District, for example. ***Uses:*** ancient arrowheads, ornaments.
*I-Spy for **30***

Pumice

Grain size: fine. ***Colour:*** white or off-white. ***Texture:*** rough to the touch because of the high percentage of pores (vesicles) caused by gas bubbles. ***Found:*** associated with volcanoes and lava flows, and gas-rich layers; possibly in the Lake District and western Scotland. ***Uses:*** as pumice-stone in the toiletries and cosmetics industries.
I-Spy for ***30***

Andesite

Grain size: fine to glassy. ***Colour:*** green, brown, purple, grey, and almost black. ***Texture:*** sometimes with larger crystals in the fine mass; may show flow features. Minerals include feldspars, hornblende, biotite, pyroxene. ***Found:*** usually as lava flows; Lake District, Scotland. ***Uses:*** building stone, decorative stone. After which mountain range is this rock named?

I-Spy for ***20*** *— double with answer*

Dolerite

Grain size: medium. ***Colour:*** greyish- or greenish-black to black. ***Texture:*** quite dense and moderately smooth to the touch. Minerals include quartz, feldspars, hornblende, pyroxene, biotite, olivine, and magnetite. ***Found:*** common in cross-cutting dykes and sills; south-west England, North Wales, Yorkshire, the Lake District, Scotland. ***Uses:*** building and decorative stone.
I-Spy for ***10***

Basalt

Grain size: fine. ***Colour:*** grey-black to black. ***Texture:*** dense and relatively smooth to the touch; there may be small crystals of olivine in the fine mass. Minerals include feldspars, pyroxene, olivine, and magnetite. ***Found:*** the most common lava; occurs as flows which may cool to form columns; south-west England, North Wales, Yorkshire, the Lake District, Scotland. ***Uses:*** building and decorative stone; memorial and grave stones.

*I-Spy for **10***

Ropy lava

Basaltic lavas may occur as volcanic flows or as widespread sheets. The top surface of the lava may look like rope (pahoehoe) or it may be rough, blocky, and cindery (aa). Where the lava has been erupted into water, rounded, pillow-like structures are commonplace. ***Found:*** North Wales, Scotland. ***Uses:*** road stone, ornaments.

*I-Spy **30** for any one of pahoehoe, aa, or pillow lava*

Volcanic ash/tuff, Volcanic bombs

Explosive volcanoes produce clouds of rock fragments and dust. If this material remains loose, it is called an ash; if it is welded or consolidated, it is known as a tuff. Both may be layered or graded (ie coarse to fine). Fragments over 64 mm in diameter, that are elliptical or spindle-like in shape and have a 'bubble-rich' interior, are known as bombs.

*I-Spy **20** for any one of ash, tuff, or bomb*

Rocks that have formed from other rocks that have been changed by heat, or by heat and pressure, are known as metamorphic rocks.

Slate

Grain size: fine. ***Colour:*** green, grey, purple, or black. ***Texture:*** even; the rock is smooth and splits easily into flat sheets; the mineral grains are so fine that it is difficult to identify them without the use of a microscope. ***Found:*** in areas where rocks have undergone changes in pressure and temperature; south-west England, North Wales, the Lake District. ***Uses:*** floor tiles, roofing slates, billiard tables, gravestones.
*I-Spy for **10***

Marble

Grain size: medium to coarse. ***Colour:*** white to grey with green, red, or black varieties known locally. ***Texture:*** smooth to sugary; may be banded; fossils may be found in marbles that have been exposed to lower changes in temperature and pressure. ***Found:*** areas of regional metamorphism; Scotland. ***Uses:*** ideal building stone and decorative stone; it is often used by sculptors.
*I-Spy for **30***

Schist

Grain size: fine to medium. ***Colour:*** green, blue, grey, white, black, or brown. ***Texture:*** smooth to rough to the touch; clearly defined layering of grains. Minerals include biotite, muscovite, quartz, feldspar, garnet, albite, staurolite. ***Found:*** in areas where the rocks have been subjected to high-grade changes in pressure and temperature; south-west England, North Wales, and Scotland. ***Uses:*** road stone.

I-Spy for ***20***

Gneiss

Grain size: medium to coarse. ***Colour:*** speckled white, grey, or pink; streaked or layered with darker minerals. ***Texture:*** rough to the touch, granular, may be layered or banded; the bands may be folded. Minerals include feldspar, quartz, muscovite, biotite, and hornblende. ***Found:*** in areas that have undergone the highest grades of temperature and pressure changes; parts of south-west England and Scotland. ***Uses:*** road stone, decorative stone.

I-Spy for ***30***

Rocks that have formed from the accumulation, burial, and hardening of mineral and rock fragments are known as sedimentary rocks.

Conglomerate

Grain size: rounded pebbles greater than 2 mm in diameter. ***Colour:*** variable. ***Texture:*** coarse grained and poorly sorted; may be layered. The pebbles may be mixed or of a single rock type. The rock may be held together (cemented) by calcite, silica, or iron minerals. ***Found:*** in areas that were once criss-crossed by ancient streams or rivers or where the sea lapped against the shore (beach); widespread. ***Uses:*** building stone and decorative stone.
*I-Spy for **10***

Breccia

Grain size: greater than 2 mm. ***Colour:*** variable. ***Texture:*** coarse with angular fragments found in a fine to medium 'sandy' matrix; rarely, it may be bedded and layered. ***Found:*** in areas that would once have been mountain slopes or below cliffs; widespread. ***Uses:*** road stone, decorative stone.
*I-Spy for **20***

Sandstone

Grain size: 1/16-2 mm in diameter – fine sandstone to grit. ***Colour:*** variable. ***Texture:*** variable; grains may be angular or rounded; poor to well sorted; bedded; fossiliferous and characterized by ripple marks or burrows. ***Found:*** in areas that were associated with rivers, lakes, or shallow seas; widespread. ***Uses:*** in the building industry and in the manufacture of concrete.
*I-Spy for **10***

Chalk

Grain size: fine to very fine. ***Colour:*** white and grey; rarely red or yellow. ***Texture:*** porous and crumbly; often contains nodules of flint. Chalk is a pure limestone made up of the skeletons of microscopic sea creatures. ***Found:*** in areas once covered by deep, widespread seas during a period of Earth's history called the Upper Cretaceous (100-70 million years ago); southern and eastern England. ***Uses:*** road fill, lime, building stone, cement manufacture.

*I-Spy for **10***

Oolitic limestone

Grain size: mostly about 1 mm in diameter but may reach 2 mm. ***Colour:*** white, yellow-brown. ***Texture:*** oolitic limestones are composed of rounded spheres with each sphere built up in layers. The rock may contain a lot of fossils. ***Found:*** in areas that once resembled the conditions found today in the shallow seas around the Bahamas; widespread especially in central England. ***Uses:*** building stone. What does the word 'oolitic' mean?

*I-Spy for **20** — double with answer*

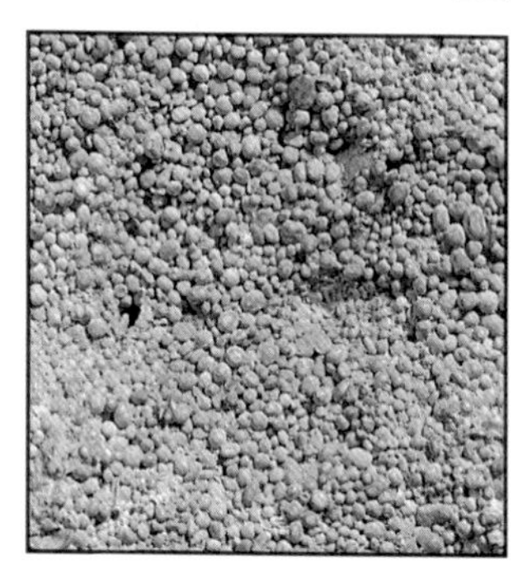

Shelly limestone/ Fossiliferous limestone

Grain size: variable. ***Colour:*** white, grey, buff, blue. ***Texture:*** often coarse and poorly sorted; rich in mud or cemented by calcite. ***Found:*** in areas where rocks were laid down in shallow sea water; widespread. ***Uses:*** building and decorative stone; even when cut and polished fossils can be seen.

*I-Spy for **10***

Mudstone

Grain size: less than 1/256 mm. ***Colour:*** variable. ***Texture:*** fine grained, smooth to the touch; may be finely banded or bedded. Minerals include clay minerals, quartz, mica. ***Found:*** clays are usually found among sequences of young rocks; hardened mudstones are usually associated with more ancient areas; widespread. ***Uses:*** clays are used to make bricks.

*I-Spy for **10***

Ironstone

Grain size: fine to coarse; may be banded, bedded, and oolitic. ***Colour:*** yellow, green, brown, or red. ***Texture:*** sometimes nodular; grains may be cemented together with calcite. ***Found:*** associated with other sediments; the English Midlands, for example. ***Uses:*** as a source of iron ore.

*I-Spy for **20***

Flint nodule (Chert nodule)

Grain size: fine to very fine. ***Colour:*** brown, brown-black, black, bluish when fresh; outside coated white. ***Texture:*** smooth and glassy with a rounded fracture; splinters easily. ***Found:*** in chalk and other limestones. ***Uses:*** to make walls and in buildings. To what use did primitive humans put flint?

---

*I-Spy for **20***
Double with answer

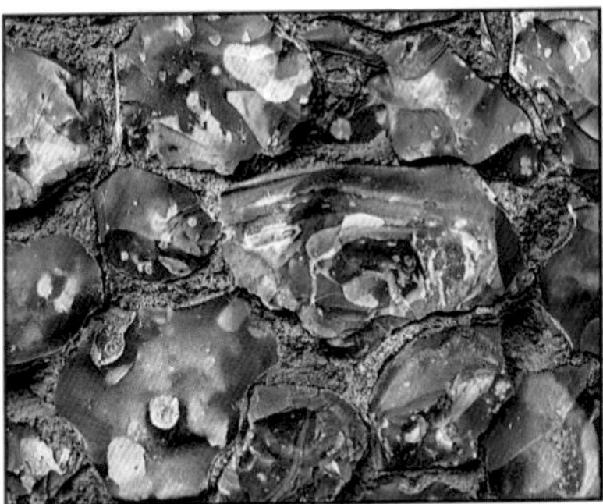

Pyrite (Marcasite) nodule

Grain size: long, needle-like crystals. ***Colour:*** dull yellow, bronze. ***Texture:*** rough and dull on the outside; bright radiating crystals inside the nodule. ***Found:*** in chalk areas, particularly, as rounded, cylinder-shaped, or shapeless nodules in chalks, shales, and mudstones. ***Uses:*** little except ornamental.
*I-Spy for **30***

Septarian nodule

Grain size: fine to very fine. ***Colour:*** yellow, yellow-blue, brown. ***Texture:*** outside rough, may be marked with traces; inside, fine grained with a many sided pattern of fractures filled with calcite crystals or hollow. ***Found:*** in shales and mudstones; south-east England. ***Uses:*** often contain fossils.
*I-Spy for **30***

Meteorite

Grain size: fine to coarse. ***Colour:*** variable, speckled to dark grey in stony meteorites; iron meteorites bronzy yellow to grey. ***Texture:*** often with a definite outer coat or crust; iron meteorites may have a pitted surface. ***Found:*** in open areas; rare. ***Uses:*** museum specimens. What is the common name often given to a small meteorite that burns up before reaching Earth?

____

*I-Spy for **40** — double with answer*

Neuropteris

Age: Upper Carboniferous 300-286 mya. ***Form:*** fern-like leaf or frond with many round 'leaflets' that have prominent veins along the midlines. ***Found:*** in coals and coal measure mudstones and sandstones; Wales, Yorkshire, and Scotland. ***Size:*** 5-8 cm across frond.

I-Spy for ***30***

Calamites

Age: Upper Carboniferous 300-286 mya. ***Form:*** jointed stem of horsetail (living *Equisetum* is a garden weed); shoots may arise from joints; stem is often ridged. ***Found:*** in coal measure sandstones and shales; Wales, Yorkshire, and Scotland. ***Size:*** individual plants reached heights of 40 metres.

I-Spy for ***30***

Annularia

Age: Upper Carboniferous 300-286 mya. ***Form:*** thin jointed stem with circlets of leaves; related to *Calamites*; leaves often found covering flat rock surfaces. ***Found:*** in coal measure mudstones and shales; Wales, Yorkshire, and Scotland. ***Size:*** 5-8 cm in diameter.
*I-Spy for **30***

Laurus

Age: Cretaceous-Recent 130 mya to present day. ***Form:*** rather narrow leaf with undivided border; veins move outwards and up leaf from central vein. ***Found:*** in fine-grained sediments, including chalk; southern England. ***Size:*** 10-12 cm long.
*I-Spy for **40***

Nipa (Nipadites)

Age: Eocene-Recent 55 mya to present day. ***Form:*** large oval-shaped seed, tapers towards tip; often appears ribbed. ***Found:*** in Eocene clays associated with bored wood; the Isle of Sheppey, for example. ***Size:*** 5-20 cm in height.
*I-Spy for **40***

Thamnasteria

Age: Jurassic (Britain) 208-144 mya. ***Form:*** branching, massive, or encrusting other fossils; the individual corallites are small to medium in size. ***Found:*** in reef masses, and in clays and limestones; the English Midlands. ***Size:*** 5-25 cm long.
I-Spy for ***30***

Lithostrotion

Age: Lower Carboniferous 360-320 mya. ***Form:*** robust colonies made up of individual rounded corallites or with corallites in contact; well-defined central rod and septa (divisions) inside each corallite. ***Found:*** in reef masses in limestones; south-west England, Wales, Yorkshire, Scotland. ***Size:*** individual corallites 2-8 mm in diameter.
I-Spy for ***20***

Caninia

Age: Lower Carboniferous 360-320 mya. ***Form:*** large solitary coral with prominent septa (divisions), and many small, plate-like structures arranged in a circular manner inside the inner wall; long, cylindrical, often curved. ***Found:*** in limestones and muddy limestones; Wales, the Midlands, Yorkshire, Scotland. ***Size:*** 10-30 cm long.
I-Spy for ***20***

Favosites

Age: Silurian-Devonian 435-360 mya. ***Form:*** massive coral composed of small corallites with few short septa (divisions); small platform-like structures (tabulae) divide individual corallites. ***Found:*** in reef colonies and as coral heads in limestones; Wales, Yorkshire. ***Size:*** colonies 10-30 cm; individual corallites 15-20 mm across.

*I-Spy for **30***

Entobia

Age: Devonian-Recent 408 mya-present day. ***Form:*** small nodules or swellings on rocks or shales; the nodules are connected by thin rod-like structures. ***Found:*** it is a burrowing/boring sponge so is found in association with other fossils; south-eastern England and the Midlands. ***Size:*** 1-2 mm.

*I-Spy for **40***

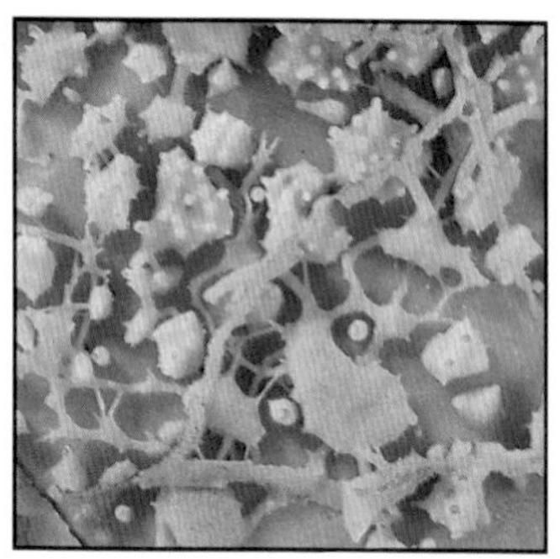

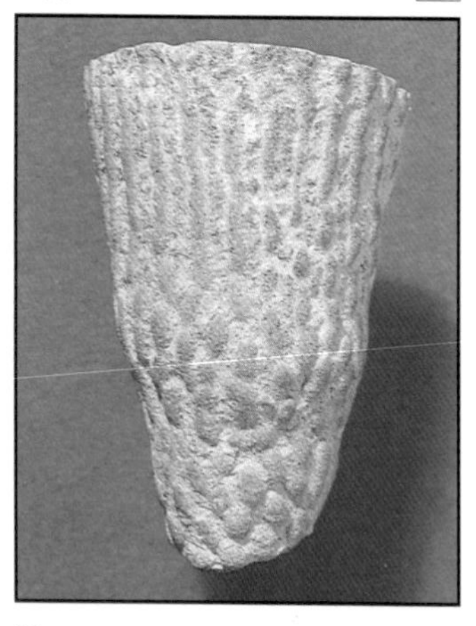

Ventriculites

Age: Cretaceous 145-65 mya. ***Form:*** vase shaped with many pores in thin outer wall; wall appears grooved or slightly ribbed. ***Found:*** in chalky limestones as individual fossils, sometimes replaced by chert; south-east England and Yorkshire. ***Size:*** 5-8 cm in diameter.

*I-Spy for **30***

Bryozoans are sea animals that live in colonies resembling moss.

Fenestella

Age: Ordovician-Permian 500-245 mya. ***Form:*** delicate lace-like or net-like skeleton; pores appear in pairs on longer, radiating branches. ***Found:*** in fine-grained mudstones and limestones; Wales, for example. ***Size:*** colonies 5-10 cm across.

*I-Spy for **40***

Lunulites

Age: Cretaceous-Eocene 144-55 mya. ***Form:*** small, disc-like or cone-shaped colonies with pore-like openings arranged in distinct rows. ***Found:*** in chalky limestones; southern England. ***Size:*** 1-3 mm in diameter.

*I-Spy for **50***

Brachiopods are sea creatures that are protected by a hinged pair of shells (valves) similar to that of a cockle, for example. They are also known as 'lamp shells'.

Spirifer

Age: Carboniferous 360-285 mya. Spiriferids as a group lived Silurian-Permian. ***Form:*** clam-like shell in two valves; hinge between valves long and straight; both valves usually ribbed; internal spiral skeleton. ***Found:*** in limestones and muddy limestones; south-west England. ***Size:*** 3-8 cm in width across the hinge.

*I-Spy for **40***

Atrypa

Age: Silurian-Devonian 435-360 mya. ***Form:*** medium to medium-large shell with slightly curved hinge line; strongly developed ridges and growth lines on each valve; valves taper to front. ***Found:*** in limestones, muddy limestones; the Welsh borders. ***Size:*** 2-4 cm across hinge line.

*I-Spy for **30***

Productid

Age: Carboniferous 360-320 mya. ***Form:*** medium to very large with two valves of different sizes; larger valve strongly curved, smaller flat; both valves ribbed with strong ornament. ***Found:*** lime-stones and muddy lime-stones; south-west England, Wales, the Midlands, Yorkshire, Scotland. ***Size:*** 3-20 cm.

*I-Spy for **20***

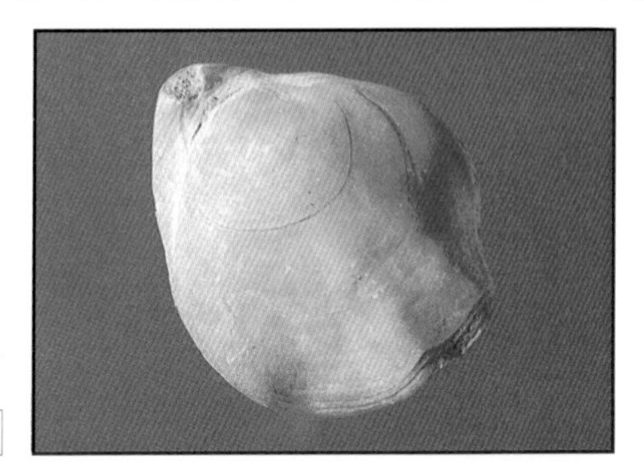

Sellathyris

Age: Cretaceous 144-100 mya. ***Form:*** medium-sized, smooth, two-valved shell; well-formed circular opening at top of larger valve; peardrop shaped, front edge strongly folded. ***Found:*** in sandstones and shales; Isle of Wight. ***Size:*** 2 mm-3 cm long.
*I-Spy for **30***

Rhynchonellid

Age: Jurassic-Cretaceous 208-70 mya. ***Form:*** strongly ribbed two-valve shell, with the valves roughly equal in size; the larger valve has a strongly beak-like development; small to medium sized. ***Found:*** in limestones, muddy limestones, and sandstones; the English Midlands. ***Size:*** 1-3 cm wide.
*I-Spy for **20***

Bivalves are mussel-like molluscs that live in the sea.

Venericardia

Age: Eocene 55-45 mya. ***Form:*** medium- to large-size clam with two equal valves; there are two strong teeth along the internal hinge line; strong flattened ridges and lines ornament the outer surfaces. ***Found:*** in sandy mudstones and claystones; south-east England. ***Size:*** 5-10 cm wide.
*I-Spy for **30***

Myophora (Trigonia)
Age: Jurassic-Lower Cretaceous 208-120 mya. ***Form:*** medium-sized clam with equal-sized valves; triangular outline with strong, flatter ridge surface in front of strongly ribbed area. ***Found:*** in limestones, sandy limestones, shaly limestones; Dorset and the Midlands. ***Size:*** 3-8 cm wide.
*I-Spy for **20***

Glycimeris
Age: Cretaceous-Recent 144 mya to present day. ***Form:*** small to medium-sized clam with oval shape; valves have many teeth on curved hinge line; strong muscle scars on insides of valves; outer surface has a weak ornament of growth lines and ridges. ***Found:*** in sands and shaly sandstones; East Anglia. ***Size:*** 3-6 cm wide.
*I-Spy for **20***

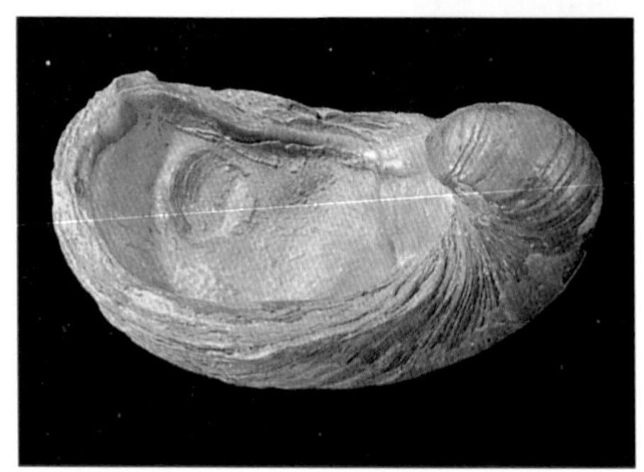

Gryphea
Age: Jurassic 245-208 mya. ***Form:*** so-called 'devil's toenail'; two valves of very different sizes; lower one is large and strongly curved; smaller one acts as a lid; strong growth lines on larger valve. ***Found:*** in shales and muddy limestones; Dorset and the English Midlands. ***Size:*** 4-10 cm.
*I-Spy for **30***

Gastropods are winkle-like molluscs.

Bellerophon

Age: Silurian-Permian 460-286 mya. ***Form:*** coiled, wide shell which broadens towards the opening; strong ridge around middle, faintly ribbed by growth lines. ***Found:*** muddy limestones and limestones; Wales. ***Size:*** 5 cm across the opening.
I-Spy for ***40*** ☐

Natica

Age: Triassic-Recent 245 mya-present day. ***Form:*** coiled medium-sized shell with a broad conical appearance; small, low spire; the opening has a thicker inner lip and is oval or rounded; smooth except for growth lines. ***Found:*** in sands, sandstones, shales; southern England. ***Size:*** 0.05-3 cm.
I-Spy for ***30*** ☐

Turritella

Age: Cretaceous-Recent 144 mya-present day. ***Form:*** long, high-spired shell made up of many whorls which are ornamented with spiral ribs; the opening is oval and simple. ***Found:*** in sandstones, shales, and limestones; southern England. ***Size:*** 3-15 cm long.
I-Spy for ***20*** ☐

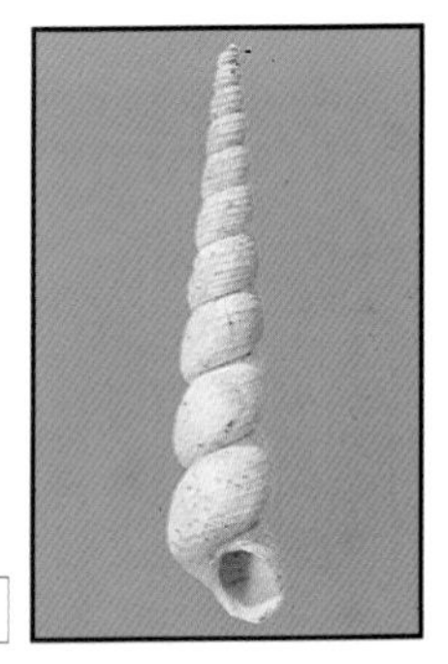

Ammonoids are an extinct group of sea-dwelling molluscs with coiled shells resembling Catherine wheels.

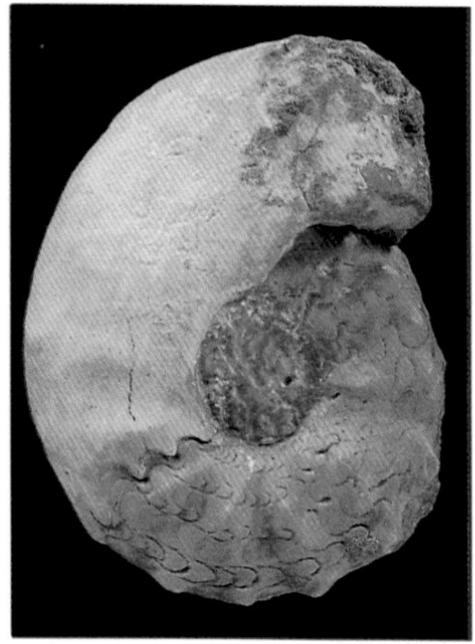

Goniatite

Age: Carboniferous 360-286 mya. ***Form:*** coiled shell with outer shell or whorl overlapping others; rounded and rather inflated appearance with simple sutures (divisions) between chambers. ***Found:*** limestones and shales; Wales, Yorkshire, and Scotland. ***Size:*** 3-6 cm in diameter.
I-Spy for ***30***

Ceratites

Age: Triassic 245-208 mya. ***Form:*** coiled shell with slightly overlapping whorls; strongly ornamented with ribs and nodes; the sutures between chambers are folded into lobes and saddles. ***Found:*** in limestones; rare. ***Size:*** 5-12 cm in diameter.
I-Spy for ***50***

Dactylioceras

Age: Lower Jurassic 208-180 mya. ***Form:*** coiled shell with open appearance of whorls; slightly flattened side on, with regular strongs ribs that split into two over outer edge. ***Found:*** muddy limestones, limestones, shales; Yorkshire. ***Size:*** 5-10 cm in diameter.
I-Spy for ***30***

Hoplites

Age: Lower Cretaceous 144-125 mya. ***Form:*** flattened or compressed shell, coiled with outer whorl overlapping inner ones; strongly ribbed and with raised bumps; the ribs are not continuous over the outer margin. ***Found:*** clays and shales; the area of Folkestone, Kent. ***Size:*** 2-10 cm in diameter.

I-Spy for ***20***

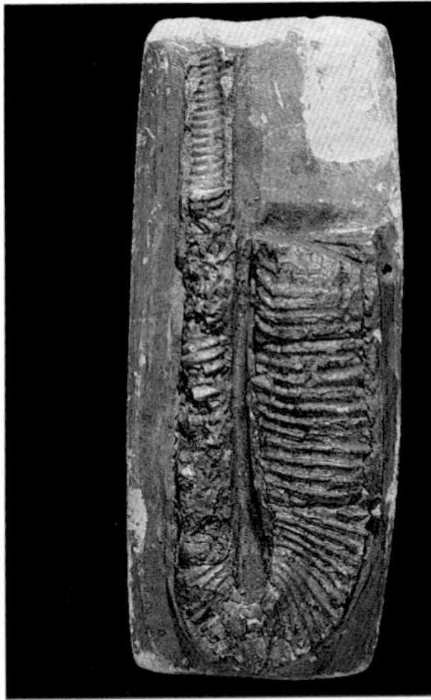

Hamites

Age: Cretaceous 144-70 mya. ***Form:*** uncoiled shell which curves and broadens towards the opening; curves are sharp and the shell is noted for the strong ribs that form complete circles around it. ***Found:*** shales and mudstones; southern England. ***Size:*** 10-20 cm long.

I-Spy for ***30***

Belemnoids are an extinct group of molluscs related to squids that lived in the sea. Fossils are bullet-like structures, called guards, that once formed internal supports for the animals.

Neohibolites

Age: Upper Cretaceous 100-70 mya. ***Form:*** bullet-shaped shell or guard; rounded in section with radiating fibres and growth lines prominent in broken cross-sections. ***Found:*** shales and mudstones; southern England. ***Size:*** 5-10 cm long.
*I-Spy for **40***

Graptolites are an extinct group of sea creatures that lived in colonies. Each individual lived in a cup-like structure called a theca.

Didymograptus

Age: Lower and Middle Ordovician 500-450 mya. ***Form:*** so-called 'tuning-fork graptolite'; two well-formed branches with toothed inner edges; branches may also be horizontal in position. ***Found:*** black shales; Wales, the Lake District, Scotland. ***Size:*** 2-4 cm long. How do graptolites get their name?

*I-Spy for **40** — double with answer*

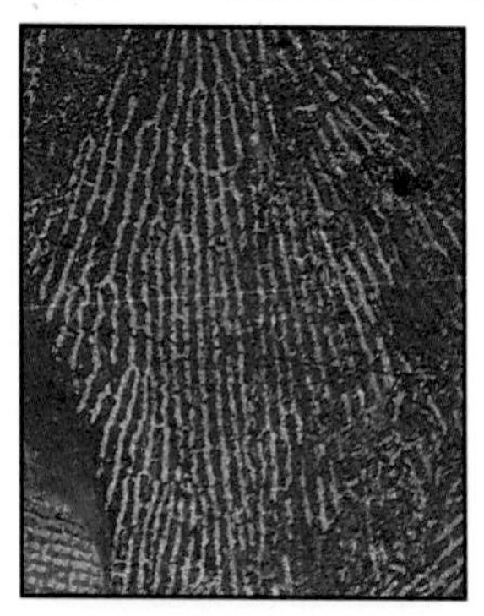

Dictyonema

Age: Upper Cambrian-Carboniferous 500-286 mya. ***Form:*** delicate web-like skeleton composed of many radiating branches linked by short connecting rods; many have 'root-like' attachments. ***Found:*** black shales and muddy limestones; Wales. ***Size:*** colony 5-10 cm across.
*I-Spy for **50***

Echinoderms are a group of animals that includes sea lilies (crinoids), starfishes, and sea urchins (echinoids).

Pentacrinites (Pentacrinus)

Age: Triassic-Cretaceous 245-70 mya. ***Form:*** large crinoid with long branched arms; stem and arms are made up of individual plates, called ossicles; stem ossicles are star shaped in cross-section. ***Found:*** shales and muddy limestones; southern England. ***Size:*** 20-40 cm tall.

I-Spy for ***30***

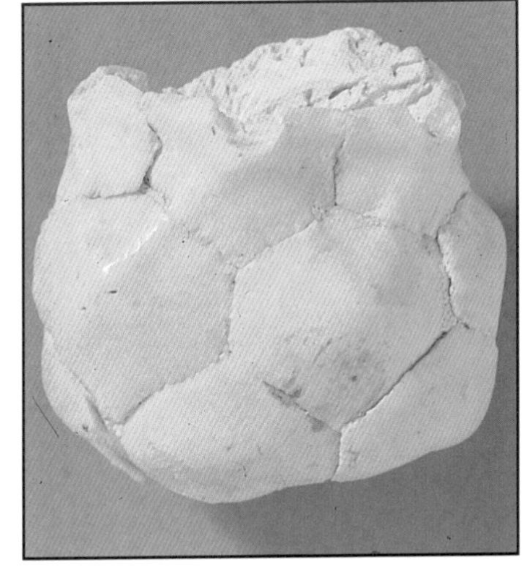

Marsupites

Age: Cretaceous 144-70 mya. ***Form:*** stemless cup-shaped crinoid made up of 16 large to very large plates; arms rarely found with the cup; plates lightly ribbed. ***Found:*** chalky limestones; southern England. ***Size:*** 6 cm in diameter.

I-Spy for ***50***

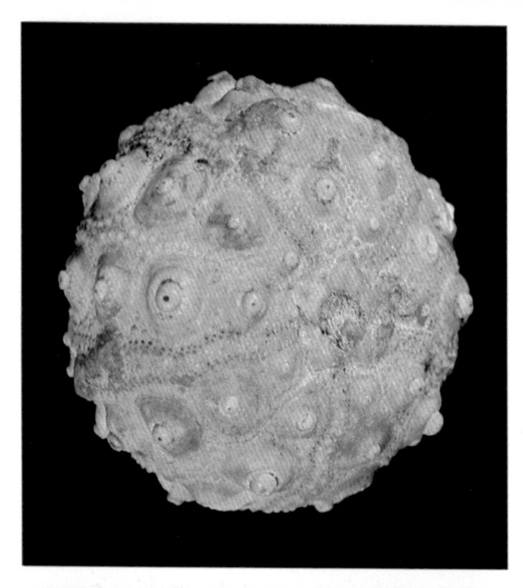

Hemicidaris

Age: Jurassic-Upper Cretaceous 208-70 mya. ***Form:*** medium-sized rounded skeleton (test) with obvious radial symmetry; strongly ornamented, with large bosses to receive spines. ***Found:*** limestones and chalky limestones; southern England, the English Midlands. ***Size:*** 2-4 cm in diameter.

*I-Spy for **30***

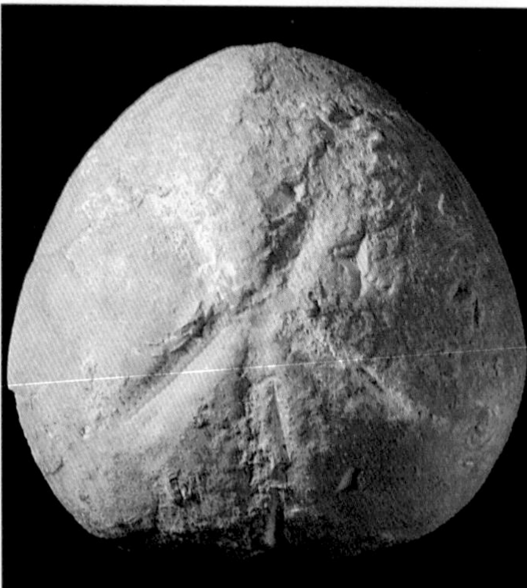

Micraster

Age: Upper Cretaceous 100-70 mya. ***Form:*** heart-shaped sea urchin with mouth on the underside of test and the anus at the rear; small raised knobs occur as ornament. ***Found:*** chalks and other limestones; southern England. ***Size:*** 5-6 cm long.

*I-Spy for **20***

Trilobites are an extinct group of sea creatures related to insects.

Calymene

Age: Silurian-Devonian 435-360 mya. ***Form:*** medium-sized with many body segments and short, rounded tail; headshield has small eyes and a distinctive central area; there are short spines on the sides of the headshield. ***Found:*** limestones and muddy limestones; the Lake District, Scotland. ***Size:*** 10 cm long.
*I-Spy for **40***

Onnia (Trinucleid)

Age: Ordovician 500-435 mya. ***Form:*** small to medium with broad headshield, extended into long spines; body and tail short with few segments; front of headshield strongly pitted. ***Found:*** mudstones and shales; Wales. ***Size:*** 3 cm long.
*I-Spy for **30***

Insect in amber

Age: common in Oligocene 38-26 mya. ***Form:*** various insects and spiders found trapped in resin of firs and pines; often sold as jewellery. ***Found:*** sands and sandstones; rare. ***Size:*** variable.
*I-Spy for **50***

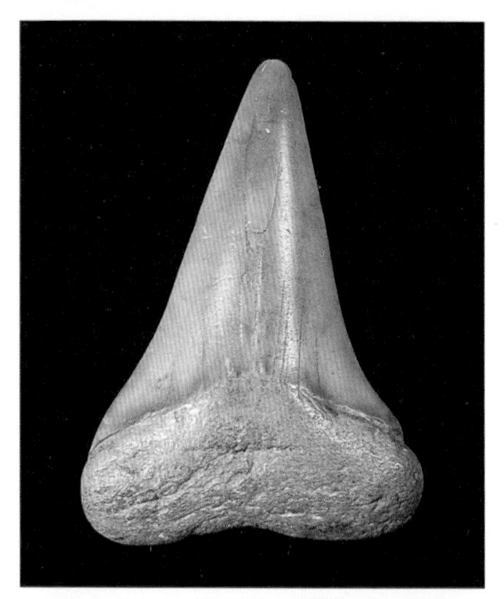

Lamna

Age: Cretaceous-Pliocene 144-2 mya. ***Form:*** robust shark's tooth, medium sized with two smaller points on the sides of central, larger tooth structure; strong, rough-textured 'root'. ***Found:*** sandstones and silty shales; southern England. ***Size:*** 2-4 cm.
*I-Spy for **30***

Myliobatis

Age: Cretaceous-Pliocene 144-2 mya. ***Form:*** broad, flattened, crushing tooth of ray-like fish; usually form as crushing palate, generally smooth. ***Found:*** shales and silty sandstones; southern England. ***Size:*** 5-10 cm across.
*I-Spy for **30***

Equus

Age: Pleistocene-Recent 2 mya-present day. ***Form:*** high to very high tooth with square to rectangular crowns; crown is complex and stronger than earlier horses. ***Found:*** sandstones and shales; the east coast, southern England. ***Size:*** 3-6 cm.
I-Spy for ***40***

Elephas

Age: Pleistocene-Recent 2 mya-present day. ***Form:*** large to very large tooth made up of wide platelets that give a strongly ridged appearance. ***Found:*** river gravels and sandstones; the east coast, southern England. ***Size:*** 20-30 cm.
I-Spy for ***40***

INDEX

Answers

Graphite: lead.
Pyrite: fool's gold.
Dolomite: northern Italy.
Andalusite: Spain, the province of Andalusia.
Granite: Aberdeen.
Andesite: the Andes Mountains.
Oolitic limestone: egg-like, because the individual grains resemble fish eggs.
Flint nodule: to make stone tools and weapons.
Meteorite: shooting star.
Didymograptus: the word graptolite comes from the Greek word *graphos* meaning writing; graptolites resemble strange writing in stone.

ISBN (paperback) 1 85671 134 X

Michelin Tyre Public Limited Company
Davy House, Lyon Road, Harrow, Middlesex HA1 2DQ

A CIP record for this title is available from the British Library.

Edited and designed by Curtis Garratt Limited, The Old Vicarage, Horton cum Studley, Oxford OX9 1BT

The Publisher gratefully acknowledges the contribution of RIDA Photo Library/David Bayliss who provided the majority of the photographs in this I-Spy book. Additional photographs were provided by RIDA Photo Library/R T J Moody and R T J Moody who also wrote the text

Colour reproduction by Anglia Colour.

Printed in Spain.